Hearts Restored: Finding True Fulfillment in Christ
By
Stephanie M Seaton

Hearts Restored: Finding True Fulfillment in Christ

Stephanie M Seaton

Published by Stephanie M Seaton, 2024.

HEARTS RESTORED: FINDING TRUE FULFILLMENT IN CHRIST

First edition. June 4, 2024.

Copyright © 2024 Stephanie M Seaton.

ISBN: 979-8227424532

Written by Stephanie M Seaton.

Table of Contents

This book is dedicated to everyone who has endured trauma, adversity, and pain. To those who have attempted to mend the voids in their hearts with whatever and whomever possible, until the realization dawned that it was Him we needed all along.

Copywritten 2024
Published and edited by Stephanie M Seaton

Preface

Welcome to "Hearts Restored: Finding True Fulfillment in Christ." In this book, we embark on a journey that explores the depths of human longing and the pursuit of true fulfillment. Through poignant stories and insightful reflections, we delve into the struggles of individuals seeking to fill emotional and spiritual voids with fleeting pleasures. By examining the root causes of these behaviors and offering a perspective grounded in biblical truth, this book aims to illuminate a path towards lasting transformation and wholeness.

As we navigate the pages ahead, may you find solace in the shared experiences of those who have walked similar paths. May you discover a renewed sense of hope and purpose as we uncover the profound healing and restoration that can be found through a relationship with Jesus Christ. Join us on this journey of self-discovery and redemption, as we seek to uncover the true source of fulfillment that our hearts long for.

Introduction

In the pages of Hearts Restored: Finding True Fulfillment in Christ, readers will embark on a poignant journey into the lives of individuals grappling with deep emotional and spiritual voids. Through stirring narratives and insightful reflections, this book sheds light on the struggles of those seeking temporary solace in fleeting pleasures, particularly in the realm of sex and intimacy. By delving into the root causes of these behaviors, such as childhood traumas and a diminished sense of self-worth, the book offers a profound exploration of healing and transformation through a profound relationship with Jesus Christ. Join us on this transformative path towards true fulfillment and restoration.

The Broken Pieces

- Introduction to the theme of the book: using sex and intimacy to fill a void meant for Jesus.

- Stories of men and women who have experienced deep emotional and spiritual emptiness.

- Discussion of childhood traumas, absent parents, and their long-term effects on self-worth and behavior.

- Introduction to the concept of seeking temporary pleasure to numb the pain.

Chapter 1: The Broken Pieces
Introduction

In a world where instant gratification is often mistaken for genuine fulfillment, many of us find ourselves caught in a cycle of seeking temporary pleasures to fill a deep, aching void within our hearts. This void, however, is one that only a relationship with Jesus can truly fill. In this book, we will explore how and why many turn to sex and intimacy as a means to cope with emotional and spiritual emptiness, and how we can find true healing and fulfillment through Christ.

Stories of Deep Emptiness

To understand the depth of this issue, let's look at the lives of several individuals who have walked this path.

Sarah's Story: Sarah grew up in a household where her father was often absent, and her mother was emotionally unavailable. As a child, she longed for love and affirmation, but these needs were left unmet. In her teenage years, Sarah began seeking affection in romantic relationships, believing that physical intimacy would fill the void left by her parents. However, each relationship left her feeling emptier and more broken than before.

John's Story: John was raised in a chaotic environment where his parents' tumultuous relationship set a poor example of love and stability. As a result, John developed a distorted view of intimacy and worth. In college, he sought validation through numerous sexual encounters, hoping to find a sense of belonging and self-worth. Despite the temporary highs, John found himself sinking deeper into depression and loneliness.

These stories, while unique, are echoed in the lives of many men and women who seek to fill an inner emptiness with external pleasures.

Childhood Traumas and Absent Parents

The foundation of our self-worth and understanding of love is often built in our early years. When this foundation is damaged by trauma or the absence of nurturing parents, it can lead to long-term effects on behavior and self-perception.

The Impact of Trauma: Childhood traumas, such as physical or emotional abuse, neglect, and abandonment, leave deep scars on our hearts and minds. These traumas disrupt our ability to form healthy attachments and often result in a fragmented sense of self. As adults, we may seek out unhealthy relationships and behaviors in an attempt to mend these broken pieces.

The Role of Absent Parents: An absent father or mother, whether physically or emotionally, leaves a void in a child's life. This absence can lead to feelings of unworthiness, insecurity, and a relentless search for love and approval. Children from such backgrounds may grow up believing they are unlovable and turn to promiscuity in an attempt to prove their worth and find the acceptance they crave.

Seeking Temporary Pleasure to Numb the Pain

The pain of these unhealed wounds often drives us to seek relief in ways that provide immediate, but fleeting, satisfaction. For many, this comes in the form of sexual relationships and physical intimacy.

The Cycle of Numbing When we use sex to numb our pain, we enter a cycle that can be hard to break. The temporary pleasure masks the underlying issues, but only for a short while. Once the momentary high fades, the emptiness and pain return, often more intense than before. This leads to a continuous search for the next fix, perpetuating the cycle of brokenness.

The Illusion of Intimacy: Physical intimacy can create the illusion of closeness and connection. In the moment, it feels like we are finally being seen and valued. However, without a deeper emotional and spiritual connection, this intimacy is shallow and ultimately unfulfilling. It is like trying to quench a deep thirst with a few drops of water—it may provide momentary relief, but it never satisfies the true longing of our hearts.

Conclusion

In this first chapter, we've begun to uncover the reasons why so many turn to sex and intimacy to fill a void that only Jesus can truly satisfy. The stories of Sarah and John, along with countless others, illustrate the deep emotional and spiritual emptiness that drives this behavior. By understanding the roots of this pain—childhood traumas and absent parents—we can begin to see why temporary pleasures are so alluring.

However, there is hope. As we continue this journey together, we will explore how to break free from these destructive cycles, heal our broken pieces, and find true fulfillment in a relationship with Jesus. Through His love and grace, we can transform our lives and discover the worth and purpose that we have always been searching for.

THE ILLUSION OF INTIMACY

- Exploring how and why sex and physical intimacy are often mistaken for love and fulfillment.

- Psychological and emotional mechanisms that drive promiscuity.

- Personal testimonies of men and women who have sought validation through sexual relationships.

Chapter 2: The Illusion of Intimacy

Exploring the Illusion
Sex and physical intimacy are powerful experiences that often become mistaken for love and fulfillment. This confusion arises because the act of physical intimacy releases chemicals in the brain, such as oxytocin, which create feelings of closeness and attachment. However, while these feelings are real and intense, they are often temporary and can create an illusion of a deeper connection.

The Chemistry of Attachment: Oxytocin, often called the "love hormone," is released during physical touch and intimacy, fostering feelings of trust and bonding. This chemical response can make casual encounters feel like significant emotional connections, even when they lack the foundational elements of a healthy relationship such as mutual respect, trust, and deep emotional intimacy.

Emotional Substitution: For many, physical intimacy serves as a substitute for the emotional and spiritual connections they lack. The physical act becomes a way to momentarily escape loneliness and feel valued. This substitution is dangerous because it can never fully satisfy the deeper emotional and spiritual needs that we have.

Psychological and Emotional Mechanisms
Understanding the psychological and emotional mechanisms behind promiscuity helps explain why some people fall into the trap of seeking validation through sexual relationships.

Validation Seeking: Many individuals use sex as a means of validation. Each encounter becomes a way to feel desired and affirmed, momentarily boosting self-esteem. This need for validation often stems from deep-seated insecurities and a lack of self-worth.

Fear of Rejection: Fear of rejection can drive people to seek multiple partners. The logic is that if one partner leaves, the presence of others will cushion the emotional blow. This creates a false sense of security and perpetuates a cycle of seeking multiple short-term relationships rather than investing in one meaningful connection.

Emotional Numbing: For those with painful pasts or unresolved traumas, physical intimacy can serve as a form of emotional numbing. The intense sensations and feelings during sex can temporarily distract from underlying pain and provide a brief escape from emotional turmoil.

Personal Testimonies

To illustrate these concepts, let's hear from individuals who have sought validation and fulfillment through sexual relationships.

Jessica's Story: Jessica grew up feeling invisible in a large family. Seeking attention and love, she turned to relationships in high school. Each partner made her feel special and wanted, but the relationships were short-lived. After each breakup, she felt emptier and more used. "I thought if I gave myself to someone, they would love me," she recalls. "But I realized I was just a temporary fix for their loneliness, just as they were for mine."

Michael's Story: Michael's parents divorced when he was young, and he struggled with feelings of abandonment. As an adult, he pursued numerous sexual relationships, believing they would fill the void left by his father's absence. "I thought if I kept moving from one person to another, I wouldn't have to face my pain," he shares. "But every morning after, the emptiness was still there."

Anna's Story: Anna was in a long-term, unhealthy relationship that left her feeling unworthy and unloved. After the relationship ended, she sought comfort in a series of casual encounters. "I needed to feel desired, even if it was just for a night," she says. "But each encounter left me feeling more broken. I realized I was using sex to fill a hole that only love could fill."

Conclusion

HEARTS RESTORED: FINDING TRUE FULFILLMENT IN CHRIST

Sex and physical intimacy can create powerful, albeit temporary, feelings of closeness and connection. However, when used as a substitute for genuine emotional and spiritual fulfillment, they fall short, leaving us feeling emptier and more broken. Understanding the psychological and emotional mechanisms behind promiscuity—such as the need for validation, fear of rejection, and emotional numbing—helps us see why this cycle is so hard to break.

The personal stories of Jessica, Michael, and Anna highlight the profound impact of seeking fulfillment through sexual relationships. They remind us that the love and connection we crave cannot be found through physical means alone. In the next chapter, we will delve deeper into the heart's true desires and explore how a relationship with Jesus offers the fulfillment and healing that temporary pleasures cannot. Through His love, we can break free from the illusion of intimacy and find true, lasting connection.

The Heart's True Desire

- Understanding the void within us and what it truly craves.

- Biblical perspective on the heart's longing for connection with God.

- How Jesus offers a deeper, more meaningful fulfillment than temporary pleasures.

Chapter 3: The Heart's True Desire

Understanding the Void Within Us

Each of us carries within a profound longing, a void that we instinctively seek to fill. This void is the core of our being, a space designed for a deep, meaningful connection that goes beyond superficial relationships and fleeting pleasures. Understanding this void is crucial to recognizing why temporary fixes like sex and intimacy fall short of providing lasting fulfillment.

The Nature of the Void: This void is not merely emotional or psychological; it is spiritual. It represents a fundamental need for love, acceptance, and purpose that only a higher power can truly satisfy. When we try to fill this spiritual void with physical experiences, we often find ourselves feeling emptier and more disillusioned.

Symptoms of the Void: Symptoms of this unfulfilled longing include persistent feelings of loneliness, dissatisfaction, and a sense of something missing despite outward successes or relationships. These symptoms signal that our deeper needs are not being met.

The Heart's Longing for Connection with God

The Bible speaks extensively about the human heart's longing for connection with God. This longing is a central theme throughout the scriptures, illustrating that our true fulfillment can only be found in a relationship with our Creator.

Scriptural Insights:

- **Psalm 42:1-2**: "As the deer pants for streams of water, so my soul pants for you, my God. My soul thirsts for God, for the living God. When can I go and meet with God?" This verse poetically captures the intense longing of the soul for God, comparing it to a deer's desperate need for water.

- **Matthew 5:6**: "Blessed are those who hunger and thirst for righteousness, for they will be filled." Jesus himself acknowledges this deep spiritual hunger and promises fulfillment to those who seek it.

- **John 4:13-14**: Jesus, speaking to the Samaritan woman at the well, says, "Everyone who drinks this water will be thirsty again, but whoever drinks the water I give them will never thirst. Indeed, the water I give them will become in them a spring of water welling up to eternal life." This passage highlights the temporary nature of worldly pleasures and the eternal satisfaction found in Christ.

The Heart's True Need: Our hearts are created with an intrinsic need for God's love and presence. This divine connection provides the love, purpose, and identity that nothing else can match. When we align our lives with God's purpose and embrace His love, we experience true fulfillment.

Jesus Offers Deeper Fulfillment

Temporary pleasures, such as sex and intimacy, may offer brief moments of joy, but they cannot satisfy the deeper longings of our hearts. Jesus offers a fulfillment that is profound, enduring, and transformative.

The Promise of Fulfillment: Jesus promises a kind of fulfillment that transcends the physical and emotional. He invites us into a relationship that provides peace, joy, and contentment beyond our circumstances.

- **John 10:10**: "The thief comes only to steal and kill and destroy; I have come that they may have life and have it to the full." Jesus promises an abundant life, one that is rich with meaning and satisfaction.

- **John 15:9-11**: "As the Father has loved me, so have I loved you. Now remain in my love. If you keep my commands, you will remain in my love, just as I have kept my father's commands and remain in his love. I have told you this so that my joy may be in you and that your joy may be complete." Jesus speaks of a complete joy that comes from abiding in His love.

HEARTS RESTORED: FINDING TRUE FULFILLMENT IN CHRIST

Transformative Love: The love of Jesus is not just an abstract concept; it is transformative. It heals wounds, restores broken identities, and offers a new perspective on life. This love is unconditional and sacrificial, demonstrated most profoundly on the cross.

Practical Steps to Embrace Jesus' Fulfillment:

1. **Seek a Personal Relationship with Jesus**: This begins with prayer, reading the Bible, and inviting Jesus into your heart. It involves an ongoing dialogue and a commitment to follow His teachings.

2. **Participate in a Faith Community**: Surrounding yourself with a supportive community of believers can strengthen your faith and provide encouragement.

3. **Practice Daily Devotions**: Set aside time each day for prayer, meditation, and scripture reading. This helps deepen your relationship with God and keeps your focus on Him.

4. **Serve Others:** Jesus' fulfillment often comes through serving and loving others. Engage in acts of kindness and service, reflecting Christ's love to those around you.

Conclusion

Understanding the true desire of our hearts and the nature of the void within us is essential for finding lasting fulfillment. The Bible clearly teaches that this void can only be filled through a relationship with God, a relationship that Jesus makes possible. His love offers a deeper, more meaningful fulfillment than any temporary pleasure can provide.

As we continue this journey, we will explore how to break free from the cycle of seeking temporary pleasures and embrace the transformative power of Jesus' love. Through His grace, we can heal our brokenness, discover our true worth, and live lives filled with purpose and joy.

The Cycle of Pain

- How unaddressed trauma leads to repeated patterns of seeking and self-destruction.

- Recognizing the signs of living beneath one's worth.

- Stories of repeated heartbreak and the toll it takes on mental and spiritual health.

Chapter 4: The Cycle of Pain

How Unaddressed Trauma Leads to Repeated Patterns of Seeking and Self-Destruction

Trauma, when left unaddressed, becomes a silent architect of our behaviors and choices. It creates deep-seated wounds that influence our self-perception, relationships, and coping mechanisms. These wounds often lead us into cycles of seeking temporary relief through self-destructive behaviors, such as promiscuity, which only perpetuate our pain.

The Root of the Cycle: Unaddressed trauma distorts our sense of self-worth and normalizes dysfunction. We may seek out relationships and situations that mirror our past traumas, subconsciously trying to find resolution. This often leads to repeated patterns of unhealthy relationships and behaviors.

Seeking Relief in All the Wrong Places: When we do not confront our pain, we look for ways to numb it. Sex and physical intimacy can become tools for temporary escape. The fleeting moments of pleasure or connection can distract us from our deep-seated hurts, but they never provide true healing.

The Role of Shame and Guilt: Engaging in self-destructive behaviors often leads to feelings of shame and guilt. These emotions reinforce the negative beliefs about ourselves, making it harder to break free from the cycle. Instead of seeking help, we may dive deeper into these behaviors, believing we are unworthy of anything better.

Recognizing the Signs of Living Beneath One's Worth

Living beneath one's worth often manifests in subtle but damaging ways. Recognizing these signs is the first step towards breaking free from the cycle of pain and seeking true healing.

Chronic Low Self-Esteem: A persistent sense of inadequacy and low self-worth is a clear sign. This can manifest as negative self-talk, reluctance to pursue opportunities, and a general feeling of being unworthy of love and success.

Settling for Less in Relationships: Continuously engaging in unhealthy relationships or tolerating disrespect and abuse indicates that one does not believe they deserve better. This can include staying with partners who are emotionally unavailable, abusive, or who consistently fail to meet one's needs.

Self-Sabotage: Engaging in behaviors that undermine one's success and happiness, such as promiscuity, substance abuse, or neglecting personal growth and responsibilities, are indicators of living beneath one's worth.

Emotional Numbness: Using sex or other means to numb emotional pain rather than addressing the root cause is another sign. This behavior provides temporary relief but prevents true healing and growth.

Stories of Repeated Heartbreak and the Toll on Mental and Spiritual Health

Personal stories illustrate the profound impact of living in this cycle of pain. They highlight the toll it takes on mental and spiritual health and underscore the urgency of seeking healing.

Emily's Story: Emily grew up in a volatile household where love was conditional and often withheld. As an adult, she sought validation through numerous relationships, each ending in heartbreak. "Every breakup felt like confirmation that I was unlovable," she shares. "I kept thinking the next person would fill the void, but it never happened. Instead, I felt more broken each time."

David's Story: David's father abandoned the family when David was just a boy. This left a deep wound and a fear of abandonment. He entered relationships quickly, often with people who were emotionally unavailable. "I was always afraid they would leave, so I tried to keep them close by any means necessary," he says. "But my desperation pushed them away, and each breakup left me more anxious and depressed."

Maria's Story: Maria used casual sex as a way to feel momentarily important and desired. "I thought if I could just be with someone, anyone, I wouldn't feel so alone," she explains. "But the emptiness always returned. The more I tried to fill the void with sex, the more I felt like a shell of a person. It took a toll on my mental health, leaving me anxious, depressed, and spiritually lost."

Conclusion

The cycle of pain driven by unaddressed trauma can trap us in patterns of self-destruction and unfulfilling behaviors. Recognizing the signs of living beneath one's worth is crucial for beginning the journey to healing. The personal stories of Emily, David, and Maria highlight the devastating toll this cycle takes on mental and spiritual health, reinforcing the need for true, lasting solutions.

As we move forward in this book, we will explore ways to break free from these destructive cycles. By addressing the root causes of our pain and seeking healing through Jesus, we can restore our self-worth, find true fulfillment, and begin to live lives that reflect our inherent value and purpose. Jesus offers not just temporary relief, but a transformative love that heals our deepest wounds and restores our true worth.

BREAKING FREE

- Steps to recognize and break free from the cycle of promiscuity and low self-worth.

- Practical advice and spiritual exercises to begin the journey of healing.

- The importance of forgiveness—both of oneself and others.

Chapter 5: Breaking Free

Steps to Recognize and Break Free from the Cycle of Promiscuity and Low Self-Worth

Breaking free from the cycle of promiscuity and low self-worth requires a deliberate and multifaceted approach. Here are some essential steps to help you recognize and begin to dismantle these destructive patterns:

1. **Acknowledge the Issue**: The first step towards healing is admitting that there is a problem. Reflect on your behaviors and recognize how they are rooted in deeper emotional and spiritual issues.

2. **Identify the Triggers**: Understand what triggers your promiscuous behavior. Is it loneliness, stress, or a need for validation? Identifying these triggers can help you develop healthier coping mechanisms.

3. **Seek Professional Help**: Therapy or counseling can provide a safe space to explore your past traumas and develop strategies to overcome them. Professional guidance is crucial for addressing deep-seated issues.

4. **Build a Support System**: Surround yourself with positive influences who encourage your growth and healing. This can include friends, family, and faith communities.

5. **Set Boundaries**: Establish clear boundaries in your relationships. Learn to say no to situations that compromise your values and well-being.

6. **Commit to Personal Growth**: Engage in activities that build your self-esteem and personal development. This could be pursuing hobbies, education, or career goals.

Practical Advice and Spiritual Exercises to Begin the Journey of Healing

Embarking on the journey of healing involves both practical steps and spiritual practices. Here are some actionable suggestions to help you start:

1. **Daily Prayer and Meditation**: Begin and end each day with prayer and meditation. This practice can help you connect with God, seek His guidance, and find peace.

Sample Prayer: *"Lord, help me to see myself through Your eyes. Grant me the strength to break free from the patterns that bind me and fill me with Your love and wisdom."*

2. **Scripture Reading**: Immerse yourself in God's Word. Scriptures can provide comfort, guidance, and strength. Start with passages that speak to God's love and your worth in His eyes, such as Psalm 139 and Ephesians 2:10.

3. **Journaling**: Write down your thoughts, feelings, and prayers. Journaling can be a powerful tool for self-reflection and spiritual growth.

4. **Affirmations**: Create and repeat positive affirmations based on biblical truths. Affirmations can help reprogram negative self-talk and reinforce your worth.

Examples:

- *"I am fearfully and wonderfully made." (Psalm 139:14)*
- *"I am loved with an everlasting love." (Jeremiah 31:3)*
- *"I can do all things through Christ who strengthens me." (Philippians 4:13)*

5. **Service and Acts of Kindness**: Engage in acts of service and kindness. Helping others can shift your focus from self to service and reinforce your sense of purpose and value.

6. **Regular Worship and Fellowship**: Participate in regular worship services and join a small group or Bible study. Fellowship with other believers can provide support and encouragement.

The Importance of Forgiveness—Both of Oneself and Others

Forgiveness is a crucial part of the healing process. It involves letting go of past hurts and releasing the burden of resentment.

HEARTS RESTORED: FINDING TRUE FULFILLMENT IN CHRIST

1. **Forgiving Yourself**: Self-forgiveness is essential for moving forward. Acknowledge your mistakes, understand that everyone falls short, and accept God's grace and forgiveness.

Steps to Self-Forgiveness:

- Admit your mistakes without making excuses.

- Reflect on what led to these behaviors and what you have learned.

- Accept God's forgiveness and choose to forgive yourself.

- Commit to making positive changes.

2. **Forgiving Others**: Holding onto grudges and bitterness towards those who have hurt you only prolongs your pain. Forgiving others doesn't mean condoning their actions, but it frees you from the emotional hold they have over you.

Steps to Forgive Others:

- Acknowledge the hurt and its impact on you.

- Make a conscious decision to forgive, even if emotions take time to follow.

- Pray for those who have wronged you, asking God to help you release the bitterness.

- Seek reconciliation if it is safe and appropriate.

3. **Understanding God's Forgiveness**: Embrace the concept of God's unconditional forgiveness. Knowing that God forgives you can make it easier to forgive yourself and others.

Scriptural Assurance:

- *"If we confess our sins, He is faithful and just to forgive us our sins and to cleanse us from all unrighteousness." (1 John 1:9)*

- *"Be kind and compassionate to one another, forgiving each other, just as in Christ God forgave you." (Ephesians 4:32)*

Conclusion

Breaking free from the cycle of promiscuity and low self-worth is a challenging but profoundly rewarding journey. By acknowledging the issue, identifying triggers, seeking professional help, and building a support system, you can begin to dismantle the destructive patterns in your life. Practical advice and spiritual exercises such as prayer, scripture reading, journaling, affirmations, acts of service, and regular worship can guide your path to healing.

Forgiveness, both of oneself and others, is essential for true freedom and peace. Embracing God's forgiveness allows you to release the past and move forward with a renewed sense of worth and purpose. As you continue this journey, remember that healing and transformation are possible through the love and grace of Jesus. He offers the strength and guidance needed to break free and live a life of fulfillment and joy.

REDISCOVERING WORTH

- Understanding your worth in the eyes of God.
- How to build self-esteem and self-worth rooted in Christ's love.
- Inspirational stories of transformation and renewed self-respect.

Chapter 6: Rediscovering Worth

Understanding Your Worth in the Eyes of God

One of the most profound truths in the Christian faith is that every individual is immensely valuable in the eyes of God. Understanding this can transform the way we see ourselves and live our lives.

Created in God's Image: According to Genesis 1:27, we are created in the image of God. This means that our worth is intrinsic and not based on our achievements, appearance, or the approval of others. Being made in God's image endows us with dignity, value, and purpose.

Loved Unconditionally: God's love for us is unconditional and unchanging. Romans 5:8 states, "But God demonstrates his own love for us in this: While we were still sinners, Christ died for us." This profound love means that our worth is not dependent on our actions or past mistakes.

Chosen and Adopted: Ephesians 1:4-5 reveals that we are chosen and adopted into God's family. "For he chose us in him before the creation of the world to be holy and blameless in his sight. In love he predestined us for adoption to sonship through Jesus Christ." Being adopted by God means we are cherished and belong to His eternal family.

How to Build Self-Esteem and Self-Worth Rooted in Christ's Love

Building self-esteem and self-worth on the foundation of Christ's love involves shifting our focus from external validation to internal transformation.

Embrace Your Identity in Christ: Recognize that your primary identity is as a child of God. This identity surpasses any other label or role you may hold. Reflect on scriptures like 1 John 3:1, *"See what great love the Father has lavished on us, that we should be called children of God!"*

Renew Your Mind: Romans 12:2 encourages us to be transformed by the renewing of our minds. This involves replacing negative self-talk and harmful beliefs with the truths of God's Word. Regularly meditate on verses that affirm your worth and God's love for you.

Practice Self-Compassion: Show yourself the same grace and kindness that God extends to you. When you make mistakes, instead of harsh self-criticism, remind yourself of God's forgiveness and commit to learning and growing from the experience.

Engage in Spiritual Disciplines: Consistent prayer, Bible study, and worship can deepen your relationship with God and reinforce your understanding of His love. These practices help anchor your self-worth in God's unchanging nature rather than the fluctuating opinions of others.

Serve Others: Acts of service can reinforce your worth and purpose. When you serve others, you reflect God's love and compassion, which can strengthen your own sense of value and significance.

Inspirational Stories of Transformation and Renewed Self-Respect

Hearing stories of individuals who have rediscovered their worth through Christ can be incredibly inspiring and encouraging.

Rachel's Story: Rachel struggled with feelings of worthlessness after a series of abusive relationships. She believed she was only valuable when others validated her. Through counseling and immersing herself in scripture, Rachel began to understand her true worth in Christ. "I realized that my worth comes from being a beloved daughter of God, not from how others treat me," she shares. Today, Rachel is a mentor to young women, helping them find their worth in Christ.

Mark's Story: Mark grew up feeling inadequate and constantly sought approval through achievements and relationships. Despite his successes, he felt empty and unworthy. A turning point came when he attended a church retreat and encountered God's love in a profound way. "For the first time, I understood that I am valuable simply because God loves me," he says. Mark now leads a support group for men struggling with self-worth issues, sharing his journey of transformation.

Emily's Story: Emily battled with low self-esteem due to past trauma and rejection. She turned to promiscuity to feel desired but only ended up feeling more broken. Through a faith community, Emily learned about her identity in Christ and began to heal. "I learned that my past does not define me—God's love does," she explains. Emily now uses her story to empower others to break free from similar cycles and embrace their worth in God.

Conclusion

Rediscovering your worth in the eyes of God is a transformative journey. By understanding that you are created in God's image, loved unconditionally, and chosen as His child, you can build a strong foundation of self-esteem and self-worth rooted in Christ's love. Embracing your identity in Christ, renewing your mind with scripture, practicing self-compassion, engaging in spiritual disciplines, and serving others are practical steps that reinforce this truth.

The inspirational stories of Rachel, Mark, and Emily illustrate that transformation and renewed self-respect are possible when we anchor our worth in God. As you continue to explore your value through this lens, remember that your worth is not dependent on external circumstances but on the unchanging love of your Creator. Through Him, you can heal, grow, and live a life that reflects your true, God-given worth.

EMBRACING TRUE INTIMACY

- The difference between physical intimacy and true, emotional and spiritual intimacy.

- Building healthy, God-centered relationships.

- Practical advice on maintaining purity and developing deep, meaningful connections.

Chapter 7: Embracing True Intimacy

The Difference Between Physical Intimacy and True, Emotional, and Spiritual Intimacy

Physical intimacy is often mistaken for true intimacy, but the two are fundamentally different. Understanding this distinction is crucial for developing healthy relationships and fulfilling our deeper needs for connection.

Physical Intimacy: Physical intimacy involves the act of sexual closeness. While it can be an expression of love and connection within the proper context, it often becomes a substitute for true intimacy, especially when used to fill emotional voids or to seek validation. Without a foundation of emotional and spiritual connection, physical intimacy can leave individuals feeling more isolated and emptier.

True Intimacy: True intimacy encompasses emotional and spiritual connection. It involves a deep understanding and acceptance of each other, vulnerability, and mutual support. True intimacy nurtures the soul, fosters genuine love, and reflects the relational nature God intended for us.

Building Healthy, God-Centered Relationships

Healthy, God-centered relationships are built on a foundation of mutual respect, love, and shared faith. Here are key components to cultivating such relationships:

Shared Faith and Values: Having a common faith in God and shared values strengthens the bond in a relationship. It provides a solid foundation and shared purpose. Amos 3:3 asks, *"Do two walk together unless they have agreed to do so?"* Sharing the same spiritual direction is essential.

Communication and Honesty: Open and honest communication is vital. Expressing feelings, thoughts, and concerns without fear of judgment fosters trust and understanding. Ephesians 4:25 advises, *"Therefore each of you must put off falsehood and speak truthfully to your neighbor, for we are all members of one body."*

Mutual Respect and Support: Healthy relationships are characterized by mutual respect and support. Both partners should feel valued and encouraged to grow. Philippians 2:3-4 says, *"Do nothing out of selfish ambition or vain conceit. Rather, in humility value others above yourselves, not looking to your own interests but each of you to the interests of the others."*

Boundaries and Purity: Maintaining physical boundaries is essential for developing emotional and spiritual intimacy. 1 Thessalonians 4:3-4 urges, *"It is God's will that you should be sanctified: that you should avoid sexual immorality; that each of you should learn to control your own body in a way that is holy and honorable."*

Practical Advice on Maintaining Purity and Developing Deep, Meaningful Connections

Maintaining purity and developing meaningful connections requires intentional effort and practical steps:

1.**Set Clear Boundaries**: Establish and communicate clear boundaries in your relationships. These boundaries protect your purity and foster deeper emotional and spiritual connections.

2. **Focus on Emotional and Spiritual Growth**: Prioritize activities that build emotional and spiritual intimacy. This can include prayer, worship, Bible study, and deep conversations about faith and life.

3. **Accountability**: Surround yourself with a supportive community that holds you accountable. Trusted friends, mentors, or a faith group can provide encouragement and guidance.

4.**Practice Self-Control**: Developing self-control is crucial for maintaining purity. Galatians 5:22-23 lists self-control as a fruit of the

Spirit. Engage in spiritual disciplines such as fasting, prayer, and scripture reading to strengthen this trait.

5. **Engage in Non-Physical Affection**: Show affection through non-physical means like words of affirmation, acts of service, and quality time. These forms of affection help build a strong emotional connection without compromising physical boundaries.

6. **Pray Together**: Praying together can deepen your spiritual connection. It invites God into your relationship and aligns your hearts with His will.

7. **Seek God's Guidance**: Continually seek God's guidance in your relationship. Proverbs 3:5-6 advises, "Trust in the Lord with all your heart and lean not on your own understanding; in all your ways submit to him, and he will make your paths straight."

Conclusion

Embracing true intimacy involves understanding the difference between mere physical intimacy and deep emotional and spiritual connection. Building healthy, God-centered relationships requires shared faith, open communication, mutual respect, and maintaining purity. By setting clear boundaries, focusing on emotional and spiritual growth, seeking accountability, practicing self-control, engaging in non-physical affection, praying together, and seeking God's guidance, you can develop deep, meaningful connections that honor God and fulfill your deepest needs.

True intimacy reflects the love and connection that God designed for us, providing a foundation for relationships that are enriching, supportive, and enduring. As you embrace true intimacy, remember that your worth and fulfillment are ultimately found in your relationship with God, the source of all love and connection.

***

HEALING THE PAST

- Techniques and prayers for healing from past traumas.

- The role of counseling, community, and the church in the healing process.

- Personal stories of individuals who have found peace and healing through Christ.

Chapter 8: Healing the Past

Techniques and Prayers for Healing from Past Traumas

Healing from past traumas is a journey that requires a combination of practical techniques and spiritual practices. Here are some methods and prayers to guide you on this path:

1. **Acknowledge the Pain**: Healing begins with acknowledging your pain. Denial or suppression only prolongs the suffering. Be honest with yourself about what you have experienced and how it has affected you.

Prayer: *"Lord, help me to face my past with courage. Give me the strength to acknowledge my pain and the wisdom to seek healing. Amen."*

2. **Seek God's Healing**: Invite God into your healing process. His love and power can mend even the deepest wounds. Spend time in prayer, asking for His healing touch on your heart and mind.

Prayer: *"Heavenly Father, I come to You with my brokenness. Please heal my wounds and restore my heart. Let Your love wash over me and bring me peace. In Jesus' name, Amen."*

3. **Practice Forgiveness**: Forgiveness is essential for healing. This includes forgiving others and yourself. Holding onto bitterness and resentment keeps you tied to the past and prevents healing.

Prayer: *"Lord, help me to forgive those who have hurt me and to forgive myself for any mistakes I've made. Release me from the chains of unforgiveness and fill my heart with Your peace. Amen."*

4. **Meditate on Scripture**: God's Word is a powerful tool for healing. Meditate on scriptures that speak of God's love, healing, and restoration. Verses like Psalm 147:3, *"He heals the brokenhearted and binds up their wounds,"* can provide comfort and hope.

5. **Journaling**: Writing down your thoughts and feelings can be therapeutic. It helps you process your emotions and track your healing

progress. Use your journal to reflect on your journey and document your prayers and God's responses.

6. **Engage in Creative Expression**: Art, music, and other forms of creative expression can be powerful outlets for processing and expressing your emotions. These activities can bring a sense of relief and joy.

7.**Build Healthy Habits**: Engage in activities that promote physical, mental, and spiritual well-being. Regular exercise, a balanced diet, and adequate sleep are vital for overall health. Additionally, engage in spiritual disciplines like prayer, fasting, and worship.

The Role of Counseling, Community, and the Church in the Healing Process

Healing is often facilitated by the support of others. Counseling, community, and the church play crucial roles in this journey:

1. **Counseling**: Professional counseling provides a safe and supportive environment to explore and heal from past traumas. Christian counselors can integrate faith into the therapeutic process, offering both psychological and spiritual guidance.

2. **Community Support**: Healing is not meant to be a solitary journey. Surround yourself with a supportive community of friends, family, or a small group from your church. These relationships offer encouragement, accountability, and a sense of belonging.

3. **Church Involvement**: The church is a place of refuge and healing. Engaging in church activities, worship services, and prayer groups can provide spiritual nourishment and support. Many churches offer pastoral counseling and support groups specifically designed for those dealing with trauma and emotional pain.

Personal Stories of Individuals Who Have Found Peace and Healing Through Christ

Hearing the testimonies of others who have found healing through Christ can provide hope and inspiration:

Sarah's Story: Sarah grew up in a dysfunctional family where she experienced neglect and emotional abuse. As an adult, she struggled with low self-esteem and trust issues. Through counseling and her church community, Sarah began to understand God's unconditional love and found healing. *"I learned to see myself as God sees me—worthy and loved. His love healed my heart and gave me a new sense of purpose."*

James's Story: James battled with addiction for many years as a way to cope with the pain of childhood trauma. After hitting rock bottom, he attended a church recovery program where he encountered the transformative love of Christ. *"Jesus gave me the strength to overcome my addiction and the hope to rebuild my life. Through prayer and support from my church, I found healing and freedom."*

Anna's Story: Anna experienced a traumatic event in college that left her feeling broken and ashamed. She joined a women's Bible study group where she found a safe space to share her story and receive prayer. *"The women in my group became my support system. Through their love and the healing power of Jesus, I found peace and reclaimed my identity."*

Conclusion

Healing from past traumas is a challenging but essential journey for reclaiming your life and experiencing the fullness of God's love. Techniques such as acknowledging your pain, seeking God's healing, practicing forgiveness, meditating on scripture, journaling, creative expression, and building healthy habits are vital steps. The support of counseling, community, and the church provides an invaluable foundation for this process.

The stories of Sarah, James, and Anna illustrate that healing is possible through Christ. Their journeys of transformation and renewed hope serve as powerful reminders of God's ability to heal our deepest wounds. As you embrace these techniques and seek support, remember that you are not alone. God is with you every step of the way, offering His love, strength, and healing. Through Him, you can find peace, restoration, and a renewed sense of worth and purpose.

EMPOWERMENT THROUGH Christ

- Living an empowered life rooted in the love and teachings of Jesus.
- The power of purpose and how to find it.
- How to use past experiences to inspire and help others.

Chapter 9: Empowerment Through Christ

Living an Empowered Life Rooted in the Love and Teachings of Jesus

Empowerment in the Christian context is about living a life that reflects the love, strength, and teachings of Jesus. It involves embracing your identity in Christ and allowing His power to work through you. Here's how you can live an empowered life:

Embrace Your Identity in Christ: Understand that you are a new creation in Christ. 2 Corinthians 5:17 states, *"Therefore, if anyone is in Christ, the new creation has come: The old has gone, the new is here!"* Your past does not define you—your identity in Christ does.

Live by the Spirit: Empowerment comes from living by the Holy Spirit. Galatians 5:16 encourages us to *"walk by the Spirit, and you will not gratify the desires of the flesh."* The Holy Spirit provides guidance, strength, and wisdom to navigate life's challenges.

Practice Obedience: Following Jesus' teachings and living according to God's Word is crucial. John 14:15 says, *"If you love me, keep my commands."* Obedience to God leads to a life of purpose and fulfillment.

Cultivate a Prayerful Life: Regular prayer keeps you connected to God and opens your heart to His empowerment. Philippians 4:6-7 reminds us to present our requests to God through prayer, leading to peace and empowerment.

Engage in Worship and Fellowship: Worship and fellowship with other believers strengthen your faith and provide encouragement. Hebrews 10:25 emphasizes the importance of meeting together and encouraging one another.

The Power of Purpose and How to Find It

Discovering and living out your God-given purpose is a significant aspect of empowerment. Here are steps to finding and embracing your purpose:

Seek God's Guidance: Pray and ask God to reveal His purpose for your life. James 1:5 assures us that if we seek wisdom, God will generously provide it.

Identify Your Gifts and Talents: Reflect on the skills and passions God has given you. Romans 12:6-8 speaks of different gifts according to the grace given to each of us. Consider how your unique gifts can serve others and glorify God.

Serve Others: Often, purpose is found in service. Jesus exemplified servant leadership, and we are called to follow His example. Mark 10:45 states, **"For even the Son of Man did not come to be served, but to serve."**

Pursue Your Passions: God places desires in our hearts that align with His purpose. Psalm 37:4 says, *"Take delight in the Lord, and he will give you the desires of your heart."* Pursue what you are passionate about while staying aligned with God's will.

Listen to the Holy Spirit: Be attentive to the promptings of the Holy Spirit. Romans 8:14 tells us, *"For those who are led by the Spirit of God are the children of God."* The Holy Spirit can guide you toward your purpose.

How to Use Past Experiences to Inspire and Help Others

Your past experiences, including your struggles and triumphs, can be powerful tools for inspiring and helping others:

Share Your Testimony: Your story of transformation through Christ can encourage others. Revelation 12:11 highlights the power of testimony: *"They triumphed over him by the blood of the Lamb and by the word of their testimony."*

Offer Support and Mentorship: Use your experiences to support and mentor others who are going through similar challenges. 2

Corinthians 1:3-4 speaks of comforting others with the comfort we receive from God.

Create Platforms for Sharing: Consider starting a blog, podcast, or support group where you can share your journey and connect with others who need encouragement and guidance.

Engage in Community Service: Volunteer in ministries or organizations that align with your past struggles. Serving in these areas can provide a sense of purpose and help others find hope and healing.

Live Authentically: Being open about your journey and vulnerabilities can inspire others. Your authenticity can create a safe space for others to share their struggles and seek support.

CONCLUSION

Empowerment through Christ involves embracing your identity in Him, living by the Spirit, practicing obedience, cultivating a prayerful life, and engaging in worship and fellowship. Finding your purpose requires seeking God's guidance, identifying your gifts and talents, serving others, pursuing your passions, and listening to the Holy Spirit. Your past experiences, when shared authentically, can inspire and help others, demonstrating the transformative power of God's love and grace.

Living an empowered life rooted in Jesus' love and teachings allows you to fulfill your God-given purpose and make a meaningful impact on the world. Remember, empowerment comes not from your own strength, but from Christ working through you. As you embrace this truth, you will find the courage and motivation to inspire others and glorify God with your life.

A TRANSFORMED LIFE
- What a life transformed by Christ looks like.

- Real-life examples of people who have overcome their past and are living victoriously.

- Encouragement and final thoughts on maintaining a relationship with Jesus and continuing personal growth.

Chapter 10: A Transformed Life

What a Life Transformed by Christ Looks Like

A life transformed by Christ is a remarkable journey of renewal, restoration, and redemption. Here's a glimpse into what such a life looks like:

Authentic Identity: A transformed life begins with understanding and embracing one's true identity in Christ. It involves recognizing that our worth and value are not defined by our past mistakes, accomplishments, or societal standards, but by God's unconditional love and grace. Ephesians 2:10 reminds us that *"we are God's handiwork, created in Christ Jesus to do good works, which God prepared in advance for us to do."*

Freedom from Bondage: Christ offers liberation from the chains of sin, shame, and guilt. A transformed life is characterized by freedom—freedom to live authentically, to love unconditionally, and to pursue God's purpose without being weighed down by the burdens of the past. Galatians 5:1 declares, *"It is for freedom that Christ has set us free. Stand firm, then, and do not let yourselves be burdened again by a yoke of slavery."*

Renewed Mind and Heart: Transformation occurs at the deepest levels of our being. Romans 12:2 encourages us to *"be transformed by the renewing of your mind."* This renewal involves a shift in perspective, priorities, and desires—a transformation of the heart that aligns with God's truth and will. As our minds are renewed and our hearts are transformed, our thoughts, words, and actions begin to reflect the love, wisdom, and character of Christ.

Spiritual Growth and Maturity: A transformed life is marked by spiritual growth and maturity. It is a journey of becoming more like

Christ—growing in faith, love, humility, and obedience. 2 Corinthians 3:18 describes this process: *"And we all, who with unveiled faces contemplate the Lord's glory, are being transformed into his image with ever-increasing glory, which comes from the Lord, who is the Spirit."*

Impact and Influence: A life transformed by Christ has a ripple effect that extends beyond the individual. It impacts families, communities, and even nations. Through acts of love, service, and proclamation of the gospel, transformed individuals become agents of change, bringing hope, healing, and reconciliation to a broken world. Matthew 5:16 encourages us to *"let your light shine before others, that they may see your good deeds and glorify your Father in heaven."*

Real-Life Examples of People Who Have Overcome Their Past and Are Living Victoriously

Here are inspiring stories of individuals who have experienced transformation through Christ and are now living victoriously:

Sarah's Story: Sarah was once trapped in a cycle of addiction and despair, struggling to find meaning and purpose in her life. But through encountering the love and grace of Christ, Sarah experienced radical transformation. Today, she is sober, filled with joy, and passionately serving others in her community, sharing the hope she has found in Christ.

David's Story: David grew up in a broken home, surrounded by violence and dysfunction. As a young man, he followed a destructive path, seeking fulfillment in all the wrong places. But God intervened and radically transformed David's life. Now, he is a loving husband, devoted father, and respected leader in his church, using his past experiences to minister to others who are struggling.

Lisa's Story: Lisa endured years of abuse and trauma, leading to deep wounds and brokenness. But through the healing power of Christ, Lisa found restoration and wholeness. Today, she is a beacon of hope and strength, sharing her testimony of God's faithfulness and redemption with women who are walking a similar journey.

HEARTS RESTORED: FINDING TRUE FULFILLMENT IN CHRIST

Encouragement and Final Thoughts on Maintaining a Relationship with Jesus and Continuing Personal Growth

As you continue your journey with Jesus and pursue personal growth, here are some final thoughts and encouragement:

Stay Rooted in God's Word: The Bible is your guidebook for life and growth. Make time for regular study, meditation, and application of God's Word in your life. Psalm 119:105 assures us that *"Your word is a lamp for my feet, a light on my path."*

Remain Connected to the Body of Christ: Surround yourself with fellow believers who can encourage, support, and challenge you in your walk with Christ. Hebrews 10:24-25 encourages us to *"consider how we may spur one another on toward love and good deeds, not giving up meeting together, as some are in the habit of doing, but encouraging one another—and all the more as you see the Day approaching."*

Embrace a Lifestyle of Prayer: Cultivate a vibrant prayer life, staying in constant communion with God. Philippians 4:6-7 reminds us to *"not be anxious about anything, but in every situation, by prayer and petition, with thanksgiving, present your requests to God. And the peace of God, which transcends all understanding, will guard your hearts and your minds in Christ Jesus."*

Step Out in Faith: Personal growth often requires stepping out of your comfort zone and trusting God to lead you. Be willing to take risks, try new things, and embrace opportunities for growth and development. Hebrews 11:6 reminds us that *"without faith it is impossible to please God, because anyone who comes to him must believe that he exists and that he rewards those who earnestly seek him."*

Remember God's Faithfulness: In moments of doubt or difficulty, recall God's faithfulness in your life. Reflect on past experiences where God has provided, protected, and guided you. Psalm 91:4 assures us that *"He will cover you with his feathers, and under his wings you will find refuge; his faithfulness will be your shield and rampart."*

Conclusion

A life transformed by Christ is a journey of ongoing growth, renewal, and empowerment. It is a journey marked by authenticity, freedom, renewal, spiritual growth, impact, and influence. As you continue to walk this journey, may you be encouraged by the stories of transformation and victory, and may you be empowered by the love, grace, and power of Christ to live a life that honors God and blesses others.

YOUR JOURNEY BEGINS

- Encouragement to start the personal journey of healing and transformation.

- Resources for continued growth (books, support groups, churches, etc.).

- Final prayer for the reader's journey towards a fulfilling and Christ-centered life.

Epilogue: Your Journey Begins

As you close the final chapter of this book, know that your journey towards healing, transformation, and empowerment is just beginning. You have been equipped with insights, encouragement, and real-life examples to inspire and guide you on this path. Now, it's time to take the first step—a step towards a life of wholeness, purpose, and fulfillment in Christ.

Encouragement to Start the Personal Journey of Healing and Transformation

I want to encourage you to embrace the journey ahead with courage and faith. Know that you are not alone—God is with you every step of the way, offering His love, grace, and strength to sustain you. As you embark on this personal journey of healing and transformation, remember these key truths:

- You are deeply loved and valued by God.

- Your past does not define you; your identity is found in Christ.

HEARTS RESTORED: FINDING TRUE FULFILLMENT IN CHRIST

- There is hope and healing available to you through Jesus Christ.

Resources for Continued Growth

As you continue your journey, consider utilizing the following resources to support your ongoing growth and transformation:

Books: Explore Christian literature that addresses topics such as healing, identity in Christ, spiritual growth, and relationships. Some recommended titles include "The Purpose Driven Life" by Rick Warren, "Emotionally Healthy Spirituality" by Peter Scazzero, and "Boundaries" by Dr. Henry Cloud and Dr. John Townsend.

Support Groups: Seek out support groups within your local church or community that focus on topics relevant to your journey, such as recovery, grief, or personal growth. These groups provide a safe space for sharing, encouragement, and accountability.

Counseling: Consider seeking professional counseling from a qualified Christian therapist or counselor who can provide personalized support and guidance as you navigate your journey of healing and transformation.

Church Involvement: Engage in your local church community by attending worship services, joining small groups, and participating in ministries that align with your interests and needs. Surrounding yourself with fellow believers can provide spiritual nourishment, encouragement, and support.

Final Prayer for the Reader's Journey Towards a Fulfilling and Christ-Centered Life

Let us pray:

Heavenly Father,

As we conclude this journey together, we lift up each reader who has embarked on the path of healing and transformation. Pour out Your abundant grace and mercy upon them as they seek Your presence and guidance in their lives. Grant them courage to face their past, faith to embrace their identity in Christ, and hope to pursue a future filled with purpose and fulfillment.

Father, we thank You for the resources and support systems You have provided to aid in their journey. May they find wisdom and insight in the words they read, strength and encouragement in the relationships they cultivate, and peace and restoration in the moments of prayer and reflection.

Lord, we commit each reader into Your loving care, trusting in Your faithfulness to lead them towards a life that honors You and blesses others. May their journey be marked by Your grace, their hearts transformed by Your love, and their lives a testimony to Your power and goodness.

In Jesus' name, Amen.

Your journey begins now. May you walk in the light of God's love and truth, experiencing the fullness of joy and peace that comes from a life surrendered to Him. God bless you on your journey of healing, transformation, and empowerment.

Men Case Studies

Case Study 1: John - A Journey Towards Healing Through Intimacy

John, a middle-aged man grappling with the shadows of his past, turned to intimacy as a means of seeking spiritual healing from the deep-seated trauma he experienced during his formative years. His childhood was marred by the presence of an abusive father and an emotionally absent mother, a combination that would leave any child feeling unloved, spiritually disconnected, and yearning for a sense of belonging.

Growing up in such a hostile environment, John was denied the warmth and acceptance that form the foundation of a child's psyche. This led to a void within him, a yearning for love and acceptance that he carried into his adulthood. Seeking to fill this void, John sought solace in intimate relationships, hoping they would provide the love he was deprived of as a child and help him reconnect with his lost spirituality.

John's hope was that these relationships would act as a balm for his wounded soul, helping him fill the spiritual void left by his parents. However, this journey towards healing took a troublesome turn as he often found himself ensnared in unhealthy and codependent relationships. These relationships turned into a crutch for John, serving not just as a source of love and acceptance, but also as an escape mechanism from his unresolved past trauma. This pattern signaled a need for John to confront and address his past before he could truly heal and form healthy relationships.

Case Study 2: David's Journey Through Grief and Transformation

David, a successful businessman with years of experience and numerous accomplishments under his belt, found himself unexpectedly thrust into a spiritual crisis following a life-altering event - the untimely passing of his beloved wife. A woman who was not only his life partner but also his pillar of support, her sudden absence left a gaping, painful void in his heart that seemed impossible to fill, a void that echoed with the pain of loss and loneliness.

In his quest to fill this emptiness, David found himself seeking solace in casual sexual relationships. He used these relationships not only as a distraction from the overwhelming sorrow that consumed him but also as a strange form of solace. For him, these fleeting encounters served as a conduit for seeking some form of spiritual connection, a transient sense of unity, and understanding in a world that, in the aftermath of his loss, now seemed so detached, so cold, and so devoid of meaning.

In his profound grief, the world as he knew it had been turned upside down and the warmth and love he was accustomed to had been replaced with an icy cold reality. And so, he embarked on this path, attempting to navigate through his pain, using these relationships as a beacon of hope in his otherwise dark world.

Case Study 3: Michael

Michael, a victim of childhood sexual abuse, was left feeling spiritually fragmented and damaged. This abuse disrupted his spiritual development, leaving him with deep-seated feelings of shame and unworthiness. As an adult, he struggled with intimacy and frequently engaged in promiscuous behavior in a desperate attempt to find spiritual connection and validation. He was seeking to restore a sense of self-worth and spiritual wholeness that he felt he lost due to his past abuse.

However, his attempts to fill the void with transient relationships only perpetuated his feelings of emptiness and spiritual disconnection. It wasn't until he sought professional help and began to process his past trauma, that he began to break free from his pattern of promiscuity and move towards genuine intimacy and spiritual healing.

Case Study 4: Alex, A Journey of Spiritual Seeking

Alex, a former soldier in the military, was left in a state of spiritual emptiness and deeply traumatized after bearing witness to the unimaginable horrors of warfare. The gruesome scenes of violence and destruction he experienced on the battlefield were in stark contrast to his inner longing for peace and tranquility, resulting in a profound internal conflict.

Trying to reconcile the harsh realities of war with his personal pursuit of inner peace proved to be an insurmountable challenge. In seeking comfort and solace, Alex ventured into the realm of intimacy. The emotional closeness and physical warmth he felt in the company of another person served as a temporary sanctuary from his haunting memories of war, providing him with transient moments of spiritual peace and solace.

However, despite the brief respite these intimate encounters offered, they were not enough to bring about the kind of deep spiritual healing Alex was yearning for. He found himself caught in a relentless cycle of fleeting relationships, each one a temporary band-aid over a wound that refused to heal. Unfortunately, the peace he so desperately sought remained elusive, leaving him continually searching for a deeper sense of spiritual healing and inner tranquility.

WOMEN CASE STUDIES

Case Study 1: Sarah's Story

Sarah, who hails from a small town, found herself facing unimaginable challenges from a very tender age. She encountered severe abuse that left her coping with a profound emptiness in her heart, an emotional void that she struggled to fill for many years. As she transitioned into adulthood, she found herself seeking intimacy as a means to fill this void, driven by a desperate yearning for closeness and connection that stemmed from her early-life experiences.

Her journey towards healing, however, was not linear nor was it easy. It was deeply spiritual in nature, marked by introspection, resilience, and an unwavering determination to overcome her past. Along the way, she discovered the transformative power of self-love and forgiveness, two key elements that she found were essential for her healing process.

Over time, Sarah learned to embrace these concepts, applying them to her daily life and slowly repairing the damage that had been done. Through her struggle, she found peace within herself, a sense of tranquility and acceptance that she had never thought possible. Her story is a testament to the power of resilience and the human spirit's capacity to heal.

CASE STUDY 2: MARIA

In her formative teenage years, Maria unfortunately experienced a deeply traumatic event that left a profound mark on her psyche. This distressing incident led her to seek out intimacy as a form of validation, a method to assuage the emotional pain and confusion she was grappling with. She yearned for a sense of worth that she felt was missing, and she mistakenly believed that this could be found in the realm of physical relationships.

Maria's journey, however, was not limited to these struggles. She embarked on an enriching spiritual journey that required her to delve into the depths of her soul. This journey involved a transformative process of understanding her own worth, not as defined by others, but by herself. It necessitated a change in perspective, a shift in understanding that she was more than her trauma, more than the relationships she sought.

She discovered an inner strength, a resilience that she hadn't realized she possessed. Maria learned to value herself beyond the confines of physical relationships. She found that her worth was intrinsic, and not contingent on external validation. This realization was liberating for Maria.

In her spiritual beliefs, she found solace, comfort, and an unwavering source of strength. She found a sanctuary where she could seek refuge when the waves of life became too turbulent. Her spiritual beliefs allowed her to see her life from a new perspective and instilled in her the courage to face her past, her trauma, and the challenges that life threw her way.

Case Study 3: Nicole

From a tender age, Nicole was confronted with the harsh reality of losing her parents, a traumatic experience that left her grappling with profound grief. This was a heart-wrenching period for her, filled with a sense of irreplaceable loss that created a significant void in her life. In an attempt to fill this empty space left by their departure, Nicole sought comfort and solace in the warmth of human connection and intimacy.

Her journey towards healing, however, was a deeply spiritual one. It was an introspective journey through which she had to face her inner demons head on, accept her loss, and find a way to move forward. It was during this period that she turned towards her faith. Her faith acted as a beacon of hope during the darkest times, providing her with a much-needed sense of comfort and reassurance.

Through this process, she came to a profound realization. She discovered that the true essence of healing does not originate from external sources, but from within oneself. She understood that no matter how much comfort others provided, the real healing process had to start from within her own self. This was a powerful revelation that helped her navigate through her grief and ultimately find peace within hers

Case Study 4: Emily's Journey to Healing

Emily, a strong and resilient individual, found herself caught in the throes of an abusive relationship. This traumatic experience left deep emotional scars on her psyche, drastically impacting her mental and emotional well-being. As a result, she sought intimacy as a coping mechanism, a way to temporarily dull the pain and fill the void that her turbulent relationship left behind.

However, Emily's path towards healing and recovery was not found in others, but within herself. She embarked on a spiritual journey, one that involved a process of self-discovery and renewal. This journey was an essential step for Emily to reclaim her identity, an identity that had been overshadowed by her past relationship.

As part of her healing process, Emily delved into the world of meditation and spiritual practices. These methods served as a balm for her wounded spirit, providing her with the necessary tools to overcome her emotional trauma. Through regular practice, she was able to foster a sense of inner peace and tranquility.

In her journey, Emily rediscovered her inner strength and resilience. She found healing not just physically, but emotionally and spiritually as well, helping her regain her diminished self-esteem. Through her story, Emily demonstrates the power of self-love and the importance of spiritual well-being in overcoming life's adversities.

Inspirational Quotes and Scriptures

1. *"We don't believe something by merely saying we believe it, or even when we believe that we believe it. We believe something when we act as if it were true."* - Dallas Willard.

2. *"A carefully cultivated heart will, assisted by the grace of God, foresee, forestall, or transform most of the painful situations before which others stand like helpless children saying 'Why?'"* - Dallas Willard.

3. *"Actions are not impositions on who we are, but are expressions of who we are. They come out of our heart and the inner realities it supervises and interacts with."* - Dallas Willard.

4. *"The revolution of Jesus is in the first place and continuously a revolution of the human heart or spirit."* - Dallas Willard.

5. *"A great part of the disaster of contemporary life lies in the fact that it is organized around feelings."* - Dallas Willard.

6. *"Jesus did not commission his disciples to initiate governments or churches... Instead, they were tasked with setting up strongholds of his essence, teachings, and influence in a world struggling and devoid of purpose."* Dallas Willard.

7. *"Restore to me the joy of your salvation and uphold me with a willing spirit."* - Psalm 51:12.

8. *"...to grant them a beautiful headdress instead of ashes, the oil of gladness instead of mourning, the garment of praise instead of a faint spirit..."* - Isaiah 61:7.

9. *"He himself bore our sins in his body on the tree, that we might die to sin and live to righteousness. By his wounds you have been healed."* - 1 Peter 2:24.

10. *"Continually strive for personal growth and transformation, allowing the Holy Spirit to mold you into the image of Christ.".*

11. *"Hold fast to the hope you have in Jesus, knowing that He has overcome the world.".*

12. *"Through scripture and Christian tradition, we see that God makes all things new again.".*

13. *"By turning to God in prayer and faith, we open ourselves up to His restorative powers that can heal wounds, restore relationships, and renew spirits."*.

14. *"God is portrayed as a loving Father who disciplines His children but is always ready to forgive, heal, and restore them when they sincerely seek Him."*.

15. *"Jesus invites all who are weary and burdened to come to Him for rest, renewal, and restoration."* - Matthew 11:28-30.

16. *"Believers are promised a new spiritual birth."* - John 3:3.

17. *"The gift of the Holy Spirit."* - Acts 2:38-39.

18. *"Reconciliation and peace with God."* - Romans 5:1.

19. *"Freedom from sin's control and condemnation."* - Romans 6:6-7, 8:1.

20. *"Complete restoration when Christ returns."* - Acts 3:21.

NOTE TO READER:

Dear Reader,

This book is a journey—a path to healing and transformation. You are not alone in your struggles, and there is hope beyond the pain and emptiness you may feel. Jesus offers a love so profound and fulfilling that it transcends all temporary pleasures. I pray that as you read these pages, you find the strength to break free from the chains of your past and embrace the incredible worth and purpose God has for you.

With love and prayers,

Author Stephanie M Seaton

Healing Empowerment and Transformation Coach

Don't miss out!

Visit the website below and you can sign up to receive emails whenever Stephanie M Seaton publishes a new book. There's no charge and no obligation.

https://books2read.com/r/B-A-BJNHB-IKGJD

BOOKS 2 READ

Connecting independent readers to independent writers.

About the Author

t

Stephanie Marie Seaton, a beacon of faith and family values, dedicated to sharing the transformative message of redemption through her writing.

Her passion for nurturing young hearts led her to become a licensed minister and a children's pastor. A champion for women's empowerment, Stephanie founded a non-profit organization in 2015, embodying her commitment to uplifting women and helping them find their voices.

As a Christian author, Stephanie's books delve into redemption, addressing real-life issues while grounded in biblical truths, offering readers a path to spiritual understanding and personal growth.

Stephanie's journey is one of faith, family, and redemption, as she spreads her message through her books, speaking engagements, and her new TV show, the "Stephanie M Seaton Sunday Show," airing on her YouTube channel. Join her as she inspires and uplifts through the power of storytelling and faith.

Read more at www.amazon.com/author/stephaniemseaton.